Fighter Jets

WITHDRAWN

Laura K. Murray

seedlings

CREATIVE EDUCATION • CREATIVE PAPERBACKS

Published by Creative Education and Creative Paperbacks
P.O. Box 227, Mankato, Minnesota 56002
Creative Education and Creative Paperbacks
are imprints of The Creative Company
www.thecreativecompany.us

Design by Ellen Huber; production by Travis Green
Art direction by Rita Marshall
Printed in the United States of America

Photographs by Corbis (Stocktrek Images, US Air Force-
digital version c/Science Faction, Philip Wallick), Dreamstime
(Doraclub, Tom Dowd, Joyfull, Parawat Isarangura Na
Ayudhaya, Trosamange), Getty Images (Stocktrek Images),
iStockphoto (fotoVoyager, RASimon, rusm), Shutterstock
(David P. Lewis, Ufulum), SuperStock (age fotostock, Stocktrek
Images), Thinkstock (Stockbyte)

Library of Congress Cataloging-in-Publication Data
Murray, Laura K.
Fighter jets / Laura K. Murray.
p. cm. — (Seedlings)
Includes index.
Summary: A kindergarten-level introduction to fighter
jets, covering their pilots, weapons, role in battle, and such
defining features as their wings.
ISBN 978-1-60818-663-1 (hardcover)
ISBN 978-1-62832-248-4 (pbk)
ISBN 978-1-56660-677-6 (eBook)
1. Fighter planes—Juvenile literature. I. Title.

UG1242.F5M867 2016
623.74'64—dc23   2015007564

CCSS: RI.K.1, 2, 3, 4, 5, 6, 7; RI.1.1,
2, 3, 4, 5, 6, 7; RF.K.1, 3; RF.1.1

First Edition HC 9 8 7 6 5 4 3 2 1
First Edition PBK 9 8 7 6 5 4 3 2 1

TABLE OF CONTENTS

Time to fly!

Fast fighter jets are
military airplanes.
They fight other planes.

Two wings stick out from the body of a jet. The back of the plane is called the tail.

Fighter jets have guns and other weapons.

Some weapons are under the wings.

A pilot flies
a fighter jet.

Sometimes a
gunner fires
the weapons.

Fighter jets take
off quickly!

They try to fly faster
than other planes.

A fighter jet zooms through the air.

It turns and
dives. It shoots
at targets.

Go, fighter jet, go!

Picture a Fighter Jet

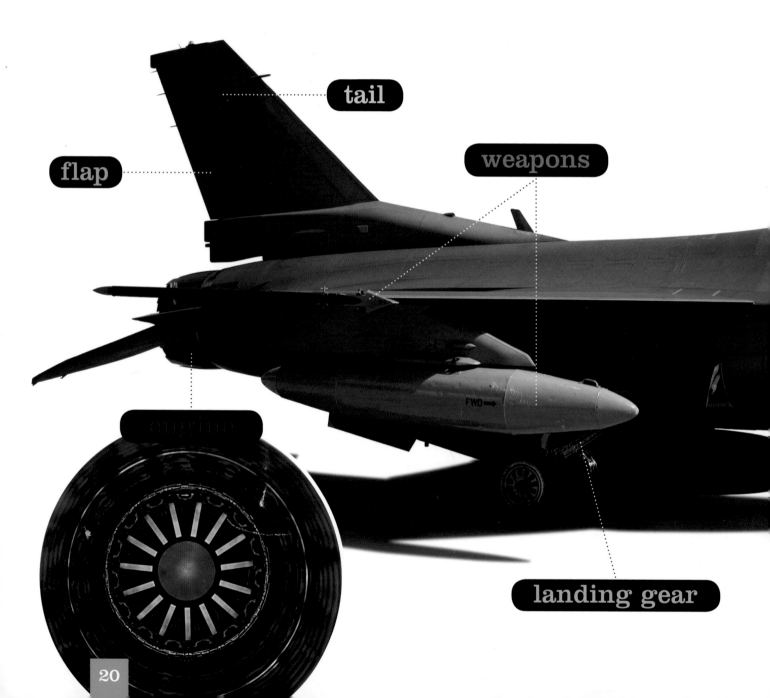

tail

flap

weapons

engine

landing gear

cockpit

nose

wheel

Words to Know

body: the main part of something

pilot: the person in charge of flying a fighter jet

targets: planes or other things that get shot at

weapons: things like guns or bombs used to guard or hurt others

Read More

Alvarez, Carlos. *F/A-18E/F Super Hornets*.
Minneapolis: Bellwether Media, 2010.

Von Finn, Denny. *F-22 Raptors*.
Minneapolis: Bellwether Media, 2013.

Websites

Aircraft Coloring Pages
http://www.edupics.com/coloring-pages-aircrafts-c180.html
Print pictures of fighter jets and other airplanes to color.

Flying with the Blue Angels
http://boyslife.org/video-audio/34031
/flying-with-the-blue-angels/
Watch a video from the seat of a fighter jet.

Index